MY TRAVELOGUES

by

Agesin Eyitayo Omololu

MY TRAVELOGUES

COPYRIGHT © 2021 BY AGESIN EYITAYO OMOLOLU

ISBN: 9798491050710

Table of Contents

PREFACE

The importance and relevance of travelling cannot be overemphasized. This book of poems is a collection of my thoughts and experiences as I travel through towns and places outside of my own country. We are encouraged to travel and visit places to jolt us from our silent inertia to realms of enlightenment and relaxation.

POEMS

KIGALI SURBUBS

Hilly contours, Painted green

Shining habitation, atop hills

Sprinkled abode, above elevations

Manacled hills, carpeted green

Straight roads, following hilltops

Villus-like lake, sustaining populations

Terraced farming, organized to feed

Identical houses, deliberate planning

Red-roofs surpass blue habitation

Green-trees, amidst housing suburbs

Expansive fields, doting landscapes

Clean suburb, organized milieu.

WB220 Rwanda air
18/04/21

NO ONE WOULD HAVE THOUGHT

No one

Would have thought

That uneven hilly landscape

Would be habitable

No one

Would have thought

That erosion excuses

Would not be the bane

No one

Would have thought

That beautiful aesthetics

Would rough landscape bring

No one

Would have thought

That long years of conflict and hatred

Would yield loving embrace

No one

Would have thought

That clean serene environ

Would apparently wasted milieu attract

No one

Would have thought

That hopelessly despairing year

Would come to a grim end

No one

Would have thought

That a future progressive and assuring

Would be engendered

No one

Would have thought

Rwanda!

In Kigali
20/04/21

ETCHED STONES OF KIGALI

Stones

Red granites

Cut atop hills

Built by crafty masons

As embankments for falling rocks

Bulwark for mudslides

Rocks

Hardened sedimentary

Hewned from rock buffs

Set on muddy surfaces

To solidify thoroughfares

Support for shifty soil

Boulders

Metamorphic igneous

Sliced from protuberation

Décor for walls and waterways

For aesthetics and drainage control

Etched slabs hailing the future

In Kigali (22/04/21)

KIGALI STREETS

I am yet to see dirt

Helplessly clinging to road sides

Cellophane rejects thrown on the road

Soft drink plastic lying aground

Food wastes dropped on side walks

I am yet to see a house

Without plants for aesthetics

Without foliage to beautify

With flowers begging to be trimmed

Abandoned in darkness with no water

I am yet to see thoroughfares

Yearning for asphalt tarmac

Caving road needing gutters

Walking men asking for side walks

Sewage system oozing stenches

I am yet to see landscapes

Set without stone embankments

Terrace left to Mother Nature

Inundating life with grassy embrace

Giving green hope in despair

Like Kigali

In Kigali
23/04/21

THE GREEN WET LANDS OF KIGALI

Habitation set on the highlands

Supported by straight roads

Linear settlements follow the thoroughfare

A relief from water and erosion

Carpet like farms inundate the flatlands

An escape from perennial floods

Hunger is battled head on

For prosperity and energy

Water hyacinth cohabits with water lilies

As humidity yearns for a lift

Myriads of standing trees enlisted

To battle wind and gnawing erosion

Wetlands remain a necessity for climate control

Preponderance of water and greens

Scorching heat stands embattled

Cool milieu frightens humid heat

WB483 Rwanda air
1/5/21

TAKING OFF FROM BUJUMBURA
-RIDING OVER LAKE TANGANYIKA

Expansive water

Bluish endless liquid

The plane turned in the direction of Kigali

Atop the seemingly winking Tanganyika

Mounting fears amidst hope

Yet Kigali is just a stone throw

Surrounding lands inundated

Overwhelmed with the water of the Lake

Sprinkled zincs defined by water

Green carpeted farmland restricted

Visible meandering tributaries

Consenciously supplying water

The craft climbed to high altitude

Far above the migrating clouds

Green mountains remain visible

Under the transparent cloud

White cumulous clouds disappears

To reveal pockets of terrace farmlands

I yearn to touch the land relief

As etched by the infallible creator

No man could have carved such a relief

But the master sculptor of the universe

Suddenly Kigali appears in the distance

As the Villus-like waters beckoned us come

WB483
1/5/21

LANDING IN KIGALI

Our craft jerked and shudders

To reduce speed

The plane tyres popped out

As Kigali suburbs appears below

Red roofs prevail on blue abodes

And the black tarmac appears

With an assuring thud

The plan landed and kept running

A barrage of wind resists the plane

Balanced aground we behold the watch tower

Other parked planes remain visible

As our craft taxied to park

Air traffic officer frantically waves

Giving direction to parking planes

Haulage transport moves toward us

As fire vehicle waited close engine revving

Two conveyance buses advance our direction

Mobilizing men for evacuation or welcome

WB483
1/5/21

MY STONE WALL

Red stone walls

Etched from the mountains

Built by skilful restoring masons

Supported by pillars

To prevent mudslides

Crawling creepers invade my wall

Competing to recover Kigali, Rwanda

Tamed creepers to engender aesthetic beauty

Burnt bricks sit atop my stone

It may there sitted for eons

Protected from water and mud

The stone is a panacea from decay and debility

Cascading wall

Erected to guard the terrain

Entering Kigali Rwanda 2nd time
1/5/21

KIGALI

Black asphalted road

Diligently marked lines

With zebra crossings

Sidewalk paved with tiles

Grasses mowed aground

Abundant green trees planted

Ornamented palm trees

Beautifully tamed flowers

Creeping plants on wall

Red bricks preponderant

Embellishing the natural order

City landscape left as met

For natural order to prevail

In the streets of Kigali
1/5/21

SHINING RIVER

The sun came to setting

Above the Tanganyika lake

The waters came alive stalking

Clawing at the sun rays

Erstwhile cloud converging

To lighten the dark clouds

Distant Congo hills disappearing

Under its blinding reflection

Surrounding vegetation dancing

Blinded by yellowish rays

Warm resource from above shining

Structures fading to hazy obscurity

Tonsils of future hope dancing

As shrapnel of wavy rays are jumping

At the balcony of Best Hilltop Hotel, Bujumbura
26/04/21

BUJUMBURA AT NIGHT (From Mountain top –Best Hilltop Hotel)

Darkness is a gossip

Bearing tales of Bujumbura's borders

The invisibles of daylight

Is visible in the distance

The town is bathed in colours

Admixture of white and cream

Towers need no introduction

For sparse crimson light dotted high places

The expanse of the city's dimension

Is better seen on my hilltop

Only that the serenity of Lake Tanganyika

Creates a void between the hills and the city

Bujumbura lies on the fringe of the lake

That Nile benefactor must be grateful for

At the balcony of my hotel room in Bujumbura
27/04/21

EXTENDED HORIZON

Extended horizon

Aquatic corridor

Pretended unison

Athletic contour

Pre-empted vision

Climatic parlour

Distended version

Didactic monitor

Double-ended garrison

Hypnotic vendor

Blended comparison

Holistic harbour

Open ended unison

Enigmatic splendour

Crowded season

Phlegmatic candour

Branded colour

Communalistic exterior

*Tanganyika River —a sight from the balcony of my
hotel room 28/04/21*

CONGO HILLS

Setting bounds

Strapping buffs

Strong buffer

Standing berserk

Shoving blues

Separating borough

Splendid brilliance

Spurious banters

Spastic boulders

Serene Beauty!

Congo hills from Best Hilltop hotel elevation in

Bujumbura

29/04/21

BUJUMBURA HASSLES

I peeped in, in April

In the season of rains

Covid-19 beckons for my status

Seven tests carried out in a week

Severed in Quarantine hotels

The populace must not be infected

Men scamper on the verge of the Tanganyika

As the lake overflows its bounds

Wide roads without drainage

That lowland flooding will not permit

Admixture of rich and poor

Yet the highland harbours the wealthy

Selective vapour rise aground

Leaving larger realms cool and silent

Tanganyika merges with the clouds

Enigmatic concerns for watchers

Bujumbura burns with hope

That organized psyche must resolve

On Bujumbura street
28/04/21

EVERFLOWING LAKE

Tanganyika bubbles

Like a constant ripple

Appearing like a trifle

The ebbing needs no shuffle

Tanganyika giggles

To edge the tiny hassles

Gatumba's pain is ample

And cannot show a dimple

Tanganyika whistles

With the carriage of skilled ensemble

Ebbing loud enough to cover the sounding rifle

Deep enigmatic water sprouting in the middle

Tanganyika sizzles

As its edges whistles

My shocking eyes turned purple

At the fearful advances of the ebbing riddle

Visiting the deep expansive Lake Tanganyika
30/04/21

BUJUMBURA HIGHLANDS

Preponderance of trees

Long decorated fences

Wide endangered tarmacs

Narrow en-stoned drainage

Creeping vegetation on walls

Dancing legumes in disarray

Wild weeds untamed

Master plan going berserk

Preponderance of stone architecture

Yearning for dexterous skills

Glass entrances, translucent windows

Without fear of impish illegal entry

Humble men, women with low cuts

Hoards of hopeful humans

Runners squirm to scale the hill

Heights manacled to mother earth

Driving up the hill of Bujumbura
30/04/21

BURUNDI-CONGO BORDER

High veldts

Open grassland

Expansive wet lands

Entrapped water hyacinth

Preponderance of brown cows

Cattle feeds carried on bicycles

Gatumba's habitation snatched

Erstwhile fishing abode inundated

Intermittent police presence

Confirms nearness to the border

Long unending black tarmac

Until Congo's national flag beckoned us come!

Visiting Burundi/Congo border -in Bujumbura
30/04/2021

NIGERIA'S BURUNDI AMBASSADOR'S RESIDENCE

High perimeter walls beckons

Wide zigzag stair cases

Sculptured in ornamental stones

Red granites of the mountain

Beautifully cascaded courtyard

Embellished with corral foliages

Ambassadorial carriage engendered

Pleasant diplomatic airs enamelled

Swimming pool atop cemented elevation

Attesting to the skill of a Burundi architect

Heart rending sights to behold

At the ornamented frontage of the residence

Real projected white house

With exotic cream furniture

And dexterously woven carpet

Long drapes standing tall

In pedantic posture astir

Ambassador's residence borrowed

Until Nigeria's Burundi House is built

Befitting the resilient people

Visiting the Nigeria Ambassador to Burundi in his residence
30/04/21

AT THE VERGE

The roads are wide and tarred

Laden with stones or asphalt

But potholes are rife unrepaired

The factories are big and many

Standard structures not wanting

But commodities are scarce and dear

The horticultural efforts are rife and visible

Pockets of flowers and trees

But public works needs more help

The transportation system runs everywhere

Buses and bicycles have their day

But hoards of citizens gather at bus stops

The city is wide and expansive

Panting possibilities yearns for intervention

But politicians are engrossed with possession

Bujumbura, Burundi
1/05/21

BUJUMBURA MORNING EXERCISE

Awakened by warlike songs

Beneath the orchards below

My temporary abode constructed

On the ascent of a hill

I peeped silently to see

Who at dawn came out

Energetically marching and singing

To disarm my panting leisure

Under the trees I see colours

Admixture of sport wears beaming

And all in enthusiastic age and gender

Stretching their latent whims

I saw myriads of gallant youths

Tensioning their body and mind

To challenge the lethargy of yesterday

And awake the giants of tomorrow

Best Hilltop Hotel room
01/05/21

FEARFUL COMPARISON (Tanganyika Lake and clouds seen in the plane)

Sea of clouds suspended

Expansive bluish embrace

Sea of water ebbing

Clouds standing on a firmament

Pervasive sea milieu

Clouds of wavy solvent

Sun rays beaming

Illuminating the terrain

Sun rays engliters the waters

Blinding stretches of cloud

The horizon is yet defined

Blinding waves without end

WB220 Rwanda air
2/5/21

AIRPORT TICKETING HALL

The hall was packed full

Filled almost to the brim

Yet the air was colder than cool

To contain the influx of human cream

Travelers thronged the floor

With bags and baggage strewn

Touts had a field day beyond the door

And you could almost not tell touts in a frown

'Tickets are sold only to passengers' is the hint

And touts have taken over the passenger's queue

Feminine announcer's voice is undiscernible

Counter attendant protested without a clue

Payment for flight was rejected

For reasons of overbooking the economy class

The business class is incontestably presented

At double the price as it is truly a class

Suddenly the crowd receded

And the air conditioner worked in its intensity

That nature abhors vacuum is demonstrated

Despite the seeming vacuity of our adversity

Cash computer revealed spaces yet unoccupied

Payment and checking-in is done in a flash

Craft's stairs mounted for the spaces unoccupied

And the airplane took off in a flash.

On my way to Addis Ababa, Ethiopia
2/09/2019

GOOD TO SEE LUANDA

I am anxious to see ANGOLA!

My heart races on pilot's announcement

I beheld local shanties sequel to arrival

My beloved heart goes for Africa

I heard Bon-Taard frequently after dawn

A perpetual greeting before noon

My English mind recognized water for Aqua

 I perceived Obrigado to mean thanks for anything

My inquisitive scrutiny sucked in the Angolan air

Beautiful Luanda Central District aesthetics I love

My visit to the suburbs tell tales of abandonment

I have seen the coastal Aquettas

My satisfied mien needs no Atlanna

Arriving Angola from Ethiopia
3/09/2019

ANGOLA TO NAMIBIA

Following a group check-in

Further to a grim cheering

Fortuitous to a great climb

Fanning through grand chattels

Flying towards greeting clouds

Full tartars gray capes

Faithful temerity in gory cubicles

Feasting time to grab condiments

Faith for travels grants cure

Taag Airlines DT573 10:25,
9th September, 2019
On Flight from Angola to Namibia

ARRIVING WINDHOEK

Undulating landscape spread abroad

Gray Shrubs mixed with dark green

Stunted Trees in the "wet" valley

Sedimentary pebbles strewn allover

Distant ridges follow as we move

Undulating mounds sprout astir

Underground yellow grasses plead for attention

River valleys are be-pebbled without water

Driest desert in the world!
Namib!

Windhoek, Namibia
9/09/2019

APPROACHING NAMIBIA

Long ridges at the approach

Earthen mounds grow aground

Sparse vegetation struggle below the sun

Dry river beds bereft of water

Tiny vehicles looking like ants

Scattered habitations grace the airport backyard

Reeking descent keeps one awake

Congregating shrubs tells the landscape is dry

Encrusted soil reveals erstwhile muddy season

Yellow grasses welcome us to Windhoek

As we were drawn to the Southern humanity

Windhoek, Namibia
9/09/2019

LUANDA TO WINDHOEK

Cruising on a low altitude

With an expectant attitude

Vast landscape in expansive magnitude

In these manifesting years of negritude

The space in between is one long solitude

And the roads below drawn in straight exactitude

Meandering river paths moved in blessed fortitude

Arid lands spread in solid quietude

Smooth flight gave us faithful latitude

Windhoek, Namibia
9/09/2019

ROAMING AFRICA ON WINGS

Abuja is a temporary home
City of strange legislative dome

Duty calls me to leave
Temporarily for a two-week reprieve

For want of sufficient passengers
Ethiopia kept Nigeria- SAI [1] messengers

On transit to Luanda
In the Portuguese speaking Angola

The journey was made on wings
Without a flapping sound of hinds

From Luanda we flew to Windhoek
And saw no hoof marks of the Wild-Hek

---

[1] Supreme Audit Institution

Through the desert of Namibia

As Namibia came from the wombs of Namib

Another week took its toll

And to Addis Ababa we did roll

We had conquered countries on wings

Niger, Chad, South Sudan, Sudan in a ring

Addis Ababa, Ethiopia
15/09/2019

NIGHT TRAVEL TO TURKEY

Endless taxing on runway

Sudden noise like a whirlwind

Sudden flight afloat in the air

And Abuja city appeared tiny below

Like a distant night market

With rows of flickering light

Urbanized clustering abode

Looked like a recently scattered fire

With dying embers in the ashes

The flickering light on the craft's wings

Kept my tiny hopes afloat

As we plunged into deep darkness

While we stayed below our flight altitude

As the plane began to climb higher

There were flickers of seeming embers below

As we stayed afloat on our flight altitude

Balancing like a conscious sleep walker

The cloud ruptured as we burrowed through

And how, we rode the cloud!

Turkey, 2010

ANTALYA AIRPORT IN TURKEY

The pilot says in affirmation

That Antalya is a little less than 2000km.

But we must transverse the Mediterranean

Gulf of Sidra held the promise

Mediterranean ridges lies in the distance

We flew over Herodotus trough

As white clouds settled over Sidra terrain

Achonor on the ridge appeared suspended

The island of Karpathos appeared

Like dying embers below our sight

Karpathos, Sitia, Irakhous all peeped

Lying on the Mediterranean ridge

Sea of Crete stayed silently close

Ramiros, Rhodes lies the other side of Antalya

Mountain ranges presented a rude shock

Until we entered Antalya suburbs

Relief looked like geography demonstrated

Rough mountainous heights smiled afar

With visible threads of roads running through

Tiny scattered settlements like dots

Seated in the throat of rocky elevations

Until we beheld the landing field of Antalya

Turkey!

Antalya, Turkey
November 2010

RHODES ISLAND AT DAWN

We came to Rhodes Island at dawn
Suddenly darkness turned to blue
The moon still shone at a distance
Islands still appeared as dying embers
With a distinction at the horizon
I can see the cloud moving
And the reflection of the sun
Made the horizon to turn red
Hills and ranges became apparent
Rivers meandered through rocky milieu
Even roads like worms can be seen
As they wriggle through the hilly land
Antalya appeared like huge excavation site
And the hills arrayed with freckled black
Freckled black turned to green vegetation
And the semblance of laid ceramic tiles
Turned to become living abodes
The sun painted the horizon with yellow
And the big red ball of the rising sun rose
To assert itself over darkness
The plane changed altitude and descended

And the craft landed at dawn

Rhodes Island
November 2010

TURKEY TO TEL –AVIV

The mist rose from the city
And the hills formed the boundaries
Beyond the hills are the horizons
Bluish embrace, streaks of white

High up in the sky
As the city receded into space
Floating fluffy clouds appeared below
Wary clouds, overcome by wings

The sun came down shinning
Reflecting on the fluffy wool of cloud
Destiny craft floated above unruffled clouds
Sea-like silence, ruffled mien

The blue took the better of the fluffy clouds
The sun receded and the blue took over
Our craft burrowed through and turned blue
Rumbling engine, still silence

The dust came suddenly from nowhere

And the craft's milieu turned brown

Nothing became visible to identify

Atop Tel-Aviv, the Israeli city

Tel-Aviv, Israel
November, 2010

ISRAELI RESIDENCE

Preponderance of trees

Intertwining shrubs and twigs

Overshadowing residential abodes

Beautifully quiet and airy embrace

Cultivated flowers to fit residences

Trimmed and pruned for aesthetics

Located abroad for beauty

Green grasses are watered

From subterranean water pipes

To add lush to the already posh milieu

The houses sat atop hills and the sides

Set like Lego cubes on an elevation

Satellite dishes and water heaters sat

Atop the decked roof of most homes

Stone fences, creamish ash walls

The stones set on walls and fences

Gave impression of communal habitation

Asphalt Tatars climbed in and out of the hills

Ingenious thoroughfare for light and water

Sculptured embankments along the hill sides

Bulwarks for falling rocks and pebbles

Deep gorges is not an obstruction

And land depression is not a hindrance

To set the foundation of a residence

But rather embellishes the construction

Terraced construction for builders is not optional

As valleys are reserved for pecuniary plants

Peaceful milieu, solid fortification

Houses pop up to keep the families together

The tent of Israel remain peaceful

A vivid assertion of the biblical Israel

Monumental peace amidst adversity

Israel
November, 2010

BAHAI GARDENS

Beautiful cannot describe

The aesthetics of the garden

On the high ascent of Carmel

To the precipitous descent of Mediterranean

In the state of Baha'i

In the city of Haifa

Of the descendant of Ham

The magnificence and splendor of man-made garden

And the principle was to create an earthly heaven

Without a further desire for celestial heaven

To bring God down to men

Rather than men going to God

Tahaj mahal in India is a joke

Babylonian garden cannot compare

The splendor of this design

Is the vulgarity of human thought

Painted pebbles, bewitching green grasses

Set to aesthetic perfections

Incomparable to the creator's loft

Eternally prepared for imperfect men

In perfect abode of the perfect God.

Haifa, Israel November 2010

HAIFA AT NIGHT

Lights shone bright

And they came a glow

Roads well lit

Symmetric and paved

For tourists and local patronage

Street light came a glow

Adding to the monumental beauty of Haifa

The inexplicable rush in most cities

Found no expression as they drive home

White taxis looked new

While the land looked old

Yellowish or creamy-ash color the houses

Adding color to the splendor of her beauty

Without making the city monotonous

The variety of designs and creativity

Embellishes the already beautiful landscape

Green vegetation cultivated added a lush

To the admixtures of serene colour

The cool picturesque presented

Added instant snapshots to our album

Natural darkness gave way to beauty

As human creativity turned night to day

Yet the day must come a glow after dawn

To assert a bright reality

Into our fabled darkness.

Haifa, Israel
November 2010

Haifa-Nazareth mountain ranges (LOWER NAZARENE)

Behind lies the awesome man-made garden

And the enchanting natural landscape

The beauty and splendor of Baha'i garden

Cannot be forgotten or erased from memory

The architecture of Santa Maria church

Defy any arrogation of human creativity

The road to Nazareth south is enchanting

Organized order of road architecture

That runs parallel to a mountain range

Houses erected on hills defy my sensibility

Suspended roads that burrow majestically

Burrowing through two reluctant hills

I saw ornamental trees sprouting

Planted for beauty and erosion control

Never have I seen trees deliberately planted

And nurtured to glorious performance

Than at the very portals of lower Nazareth

Where men exercised their power over elements

Lower Nazareth, Israel
November 2010

NAZARETH

I beheld the suburb of Nazareth

Prancing glance will not do

I beheld Nazareth in the valley

Pitted against Pissi-Pissi Mountain

I beheld protective shadows cast

Planted fields of olives and pomegranates

I beheld Karkur and Harish in Nazareth

Panoramic view from the mount of Carmel

I beheld the Nazareth of old

Pavilion of splendour between two hills.

On mount Carmel -Nazareth, Israel
November 2010

GALILEE

Through the valley we went

Submerged by dreary mountains

Olives grows by the descent

A far cry from the hilly ascent

A Man once walked this way

Through its roads and mountain backside

It was here that dead Lazarus rose

And where he spoke the words-Tali Takumi

Nain's inhabitant and the widow cannot forget

The Man who walked through this valley

Where the dead came alive

The Man of Galilee!

Galilee, Israel
November 2010

MOUNT TABOR

Tabor stood like an immovable mountain

Different from the other mountains

Covered in a bluish embrace

Symmetrical like architects built it

Submerged in a bluish cloud

And the ascent with white pebbles

Jewish inhabitants made their abode

At the edge of the awesome mountain

That the blessedness of Tabor

May rest on them and their children

That the presence of God in clouds

May bring the Almighty to their doorsteps

Abraham knew when he met Melchizedec

There made covenant of peace and prosperity

It is the mount of Transfiguration

That pointed Jesus to the three disciples

In the witness of Moses and Elijah

Equal on all sides, a protrusion from depths

The summit is accessed by a zigzag road

Woven in consistent pattern as in a woman's hair

Breathtaking in its embrace

It is impregnably awesome

Tabor remains intrinsically enigmatic

Mount Tabor, Israel
November 2010

LAKE TIBERIAS AT NIGHT

Sea of Tiberias holds an ace

As Syria came shinning bright

With white bulbs in the distance

Jordan stood near watching

List'ng to the sounds of the Sea of Galilee

I bathed in the shinning reflection

Reflection of the Galilee waters

As shimmering reflections came blindly

From the roundish opaque moon

Blaring its harmless rays on the waters

In its unclouded fullness

Lake Tiberias sets the pace

As we beheld three nations at a glance

Lake Tiberias, Israel
November 2010

CAPERNUM

How true are you

Your words are true

That Capernaum will come to ruins

The story is still true today

The house Peter lived

Came to a ruinous end

That of the mother-in-law

Came to ruins also

Even the temple of worship

Suffered the fate of destruction

Crusaders re-erected Capernaum temple

And Saladin brought it to ruins

I found no house standing

Save rubbles and stones

I found no soul in Capernaum

Save stones atop stones

And I remember the words of the Lord

That tells He is true

How true are you

Your words are true

Capernum, Israel -November 2010

SEA OF GALILEE

Afloat on water

That Jesus once transversed

I know not either

That I will do as He did

He crossed the sea to see men

In compassion He rode the waves

The multitude of His days

Knew a man passed their land

Thousand years had not stopped men

To know the one who once walked

And the sea waves obeyed His voice

On the Sea of Galilee

Thousand years had not erased Him

From the very sand He stepped on

His footprints is seen today

Even as he left it for eons

We see it boldly written

Today on its sands and shores

While we stood and beheld

The Sea of Galilee

Sea of Galilee, Israel -November 2010

MOUNT SCORPUS

Hallelujah!

From this exalted position

Hallelujah!

I beheld the city

Hallelujah!

The city of God

Hallelujah!

I beheld the walls

Hallelujah!

And the city within

Hallelujah!

There the Jews behold the city

Hallelujah!

At mount Scorpus

Hallelujah!

There I beheld Jerusalem

Hallelujah!

The city of God!

Mount Scorpus, Israel
December 2010

MOUNT OF OLIVES

There He met with the disciples

And gave them a promise

That they must be with scruples

And wait for His coming

He ascended into heaven in ripples

And the disciples all saw Him

Save Judas Iscariot in wimples

And hung bursting in the middle

Mount Olives, Israel
December 2010

MOUNT OF OLIVES II

I beheld Kidron valley

And the Kidron river

That reminded me of the place

Between the mount of Moriah and Olives

Lord Jesus predicted the ruin of the temple

That no stone will lie atop another

The prophesy of 2000 years

Have come true here

Here on olives He wept over the temple

As He saw it come to ruin

The mother of Jesus lived here

Until she carried the holy seed

Here the disciples saw their master

Lifted high above the heavens

At Olive Mountain shall He descend

To come back for His own

Mount Olives, Israel
December 2010

DEAD SEA

River Jordan flowed ceaselessly

To empty its content at the Dead Sea

Though she meandered its way

Through dry and patched places

Dead Sea had her own share of water

Reluctantly refusing to empty hers

To receive freshness and depth

We have come to the place of salts

Where men float like on water bed

Dead Sea had received the best from others

Refusing to give anything to any one

Deadness is in the bosom of the stingy

Dry, patched earth took some

And the hot sun took its share

Dead Sea shrunk in years

And lost the creatures within

Salt contended with these and even men

Until the sea died in the deposit of salt

Dead Sea, Israel
December 2010

MOUNT SINAI IN EGYPT

Vast mountainous milieu

Rapturous inexpressible heights

Blocking the jejune horizon

Casting shadows on my contemplation

Basalt rocks rose amidst rocky hills

Magnificent eruption from eons past

Overwhelmingly huge awesomeness

Seated solidly unmoved

Climbing Sinai Mountain

To assert the resilience of nature

Moses climbed the mount in expectancy

He had a purpose and a vision in mind

Mount Sinai remains impregnable

Panting remembrance of the almighty God

Here God wrote letters to His creatures

And brought meaning to life and living

Trekking pilgrim had a mount to contend with

Climbing camels and Bedouin Arabs available at hand

To reduce the ennui of an hectic journey

And scale Sinai to its summit peak

Moses saw fire burning

Where the bush was not burnt

I beheld the back side of the desert

Where Moses heard God and prospered

Atop Sinai, the awesomeness of God

The morning sun came in its full blast

The tiredness of climbing turned to strength

Standing above my limitations

Mount Sinai, Egypt
December 2010

THE CRATER OF MITZPE RAMON

I came to Negev desert

To a giant crater in Southern Israel

And stood on the cliff edge

The cliff edge of Mitzpe

Beholding the wonders of Mitzpe Ramon

The Mitzpe pomegranate

Where rocks stood atop rocks

Eternal God work for eons

To set the earth on a balance

Men came to alter the scale

Yet his work cannot be altered

The earth opened its mouth

As if to utter some words

Strong words are spoken at Mitzpe

Without uttering a tonal sound

Black basalt erupted from the belly of the earth

As ingenuity of men burrowed through

From her belly to her very throat

Where Mitzpe Ramon seats comfortably

Staggering heights that men have conquered

Rickety dizziness to the weak and the fearful

I must rise above generational subsistence

Monumental inducements, panting courage

I witnessed first-hand the awesomeness of God

And the omnipotent of the Almighty.

Negev desert, Israel
December 2010

EILAT TO JERUSALEM

Pilgrims took off from Eilat yearning to see Jerusalem

As we engage a continual stretch of mountain ranges

Date palm plantations followed in its wake

Linear stretch of hills followed the roads

Like guardian angels on holy assignment

The clouds met with the dust at the horizon

Shrinking shrubs sprouted from dry earth

All around Yotivata and Timna animal park

Habitations of Lotan, Mizpe Rammon and Beer-sheva

Appeared on blue sign posts

Brown, clayey denudated rocks

Peeping protrusions everywhere

Appearing like faces carved by erosion

Falling rocks tell of the sun's harshness

As we climb the awesome hills of En Quetura

Burrowing through its majestic hills

The resilience of human nature is matchless

Trees, shrubs, and grasses disappeared

In the entrances of Qem, Shittim, Ramat and Negev

The whitish Shittim hills stood afar off

Diverging from those of En Quetura

The hillocks are sprayed black in Terrashim

And the emerging valleys deep

My face is set like a flint to Jerushallayim

The city set on a hill that cannot be hid

We are continuously on the upward ascent

Never to bow to the elements any more

Rare isolated cisterns before the wilderness of Zin,

Fresh Shrubs brought hope at Avedat settlements

And Ramat Negev oasis brought memories of trees

Minkoff Park took care of our belly needs

Like the oasis took care of plants for eons

Abraham's well stood by river Beersheba

We saw Gizo, city of Kaolin and Zora forest

And made a detour to the valley of Elah

Where the Goliath of Gath suffered

Receiving divine deadly blow from David

Heading to Yitzhak Rabin on Jerusalem highway

Mounting hills on a continuous ascent to Jerusalem

And our yearnings became a reality!

Eilat, Israel
December 2010

STONES OF JERUSALEM

Hewn stones stood atop one another

In shapes and sizes

Hewned from Mother Mountains

It could be from limestone hillocks

Pinkish-white, they appear in forms

In locations they never dreamt of

To sit and beatify another location

Large chunk of rock once stood

So impregnably unconquerable

Yielded to the sculptor's craft

And came to town in smaller chunks

To beautify a once ruffled milieu

The earth is a loose piece of material

Requiring the discipline of stones

Even the beauty of hewned rocks

To define its boundaries and borders

With these, conquerors have set borders

To assert and propagate rulership

High walls have been deliberately erected

To demarcate ownership of land and properties

Hewn stones have built homes and citadels

Paved roads and made bulwarks

The rock of Jerusalem is with us

To remain our corner stone

Forever

Jerusalem
December 2010

YAD VASHEM MEMORIAL

I beheld the stars in myriads

Myriads of stars quenched

Quenched at the prime of life

I beheld overwhelming darkness

Darkness that envelops within

Within lies the hope of a nation

I beheld the cement pyramid

Pyramid keeping remembrance of events

Events of Jewish holocaust

I beheld the forest reserved

Reserved to remember the dead

Dead but not forgotten

I beheld the gloomy face of people

People who felt the pangs of war and agony

Agony of hate, torture and death

I beheld my tears tumbling

Tears running down my cheeks

Cheeks consumed of passion for tomorrow

I beheld a nation

Nation that out of multiple ruins rose

Rose out of the spoil of the past!

Jerusalem -December 2010

BYE- BYE TEL AVIV

We took off from Ben Gurion airport

Beholding the sky crappers of Tel Aviv

The morning sun came by the craft's window

Telling us of the advance of a new day

Date palm swung in the distance

Cultivated forests can be seen at the horizon

Other crafts appear like toys on the tarmac

And the world became a little smaller

Colourful bongevillea decorated the tarmac's edge

An array of planes gave way to residential abodes

As the shadow of our craft followed behind

I beheld cars moving like ants on tiny ropes

And sky crappers like boxes on sandy beach

Network of roads as intertwining threads aground

And the blue sea took over the entire visage

I could not differentiate the sea and the sky

Beholding the imperceptible horizon afar

Ben Gurion airport stood afar

And receded into the distance

The plane headed into the island of Malta

And Tel Aviv remained green in my heart

Tel-Aviv Israel -December 2010

DESCENT TO MALTA

Soaring high above the sky

Beyond tens of thousands in altitude

Under the clear blue sky

Above the congregating clouds beneath

The descent brought challenges

And the cabin became darker

As the clouds became thicker

And the temperature colder

Visibility became impaired

Save communications in the cockpit

The air stood still like it's congealed

Turgid air remained in their solidity

Below is an expansive possibilities

Only explored by the courageous

Above remain majorly unexplored

If only in our descent we soar

Valleta, Malta
December 2010

IRONY OF ALTITUDE

Metal Bird, Air bus

Tiny hamlets, Big Cities

Dying embers, Street lightings

Floating bubbles, drifting clouds

Enplaited greens, Crop plantation

Becracked pottery, Communal assemblage

Enammeled porcelain, Collective shacks

 Uneven carpeting, scattered farmlands

Vast vapourization, cumulous cloud

Slippery edge, Cloudy horizon

Endless Blue, Vast Ocean

High altitude, Distant reality.

On the plane to Sierra Leone
2004

METAL BIRD ON WINGS

It took off!

With wings astir

Inside its belly

Homo sapiens transverse

Ends of the earth

The giant in the ave's family

Heaved thunderous sign

 Belched and gurgled

Then floated peacefully

I'm amazed at this discovery

Floating weight

Weighty balance

Flying metals

Soaring Eagles

On the plane to Sierra Leone
2004

SPHERICAL GLOBE

I will stand on the base

Ignorance has no place

Travelling holds the ace

The world needs a gauge

Temporary migration needs no lease

Ogling tourists has no case

No need for shame carrying the mace

Nor withdrawal for loss of face

Fluid humanity runs the race

Decorating our landscapes like the lace

Volumes of water dictate no pace

As panting manifesto yield to space

The spherical globe is a maze

As men seek meaning in the haze

When adventure beckons to daze

Our soulish yearning will find the ease

Israel
November 2010

www.ingramcontent.com/pod-product-compliance
Lightning Source LLC
Chambersburg PA
CBHW051343150726

48000CB00003B/1021